POMPEII

Ron and Nancy Goor

POMPEII
Exploring a Roman Ghost Town

PHOTOGRAPHS BY RON GOOR

THOMAS Y. CROWELL   NEW YORK

To Stelli, with love

ACKNOWLEDGMENTS

The authors would like to thank Penguin Books Ltd. and The Macmillan Company for permission to quote "A Recipe for Making Garum" on page 109 as well as the rules for dining etiquette on page 75 (*Cities of Vesuvius: Pompeii and Herculaneum* by Michael Grant, The Macmillan Company, 1971, Penguin Books, 1976), and Betty Radice for allowing us to quote her translation of *The Letters of the Younger Pliny*, published in the Loeb Library Edition (Cambridge, Mass., and London, 1969). Also, The Macmillan Publishing Company for allowing us to print the graffiti quoted on page 42 (*Pompeii, Its Life and Art* by August Mau, 1902).

Library of Congress Cataloging-in-Publication Data
Goor, Ron.
    Pompeii.

    Summary: Explores the social, political, cultural,
and religious life in the ancient Roman city of
Pompeii, destroyed in a volcanic eruption in A.D. 79
and not rediscovered until the late seventeenth century.
    1. Pompeii (Ancient city)—Juvenile literature.
[1. Pompeii (Ancient city)] I. Goor, Nancy. II. Title.
DG70.P7G64 1986   937'.7   85-47895
ISBN 0-690-04515-8
ISBN 0-690-04516-6 (lib. bdg.)

CONTENTS

INTRODUCTION ix

DEATH AND DISCOVERY 2
  Where did all the people go? 2
    A Thriving Roman Town 2
    Earthquake of A.D. 62 6
    Mt. Vesuvius Blows Its Stack 7
    Pompeii Dies at 6:30 A.M., August 25 9
    Death 10
    Buried and Soon Forgotten 13
  How was Pompeii discovered? 13
    The First Clue 13
    Herculaneum Is Discovered 13
    Digging Out Pompeii 14
    Map of Pompeii 14
  Why are Pompeii and Herculaneum so important? 17
    Bringing Pompeii to Life 17

INSIDE THE WALLS 22
  Pompeii in A.D. 79 22
  Major Features of Pompeii 23
    Site 23
    Wall and Gates 23
    Street Plan 25
    Public Areas 26
    Streets of Tombs 26
  A Walk Through the Streets of Pompeii 28

Roman Engineering Genius: Pompeii's Water System   30

PUBLIC LIFE   36
  The Forum: The Heart of a Roman City   36
    Government   38
    Duoviri, Aediles, and Decuriones   38
    Basilica and the Law   40
  Graffiti   41
    Election Graffiti on the Walls   42
  Religion   44
    Worship at Home   48
    Oriental Religions Fill a Void   51
  Popular Entertainment   51
    Theater   52
    Amphitheater   55
    Physical Fitness and Exercise   58
    Baths: Not Just for Keeping Clean   61
      Central Heating in A.D. 79   63

PRIVATE LIFE   66
  Homes   66
    The Atrium, Cool and Serene   66
    Bringing the Outside Inside   69
    Cubiculae   69
    Tablinum   71
    Peristyle   71
    Dining Rooms (Triclinia)   75
      Dining Etiquette   75
      A Three- to Seven-Course Feast   76
    Kitchen   77
    Bath   78

Toilet   78

Slave Quarters   79

Artwork   79

The Discomforts of Home   84

Making More Room   86

Childhood   89

Schools   91

Toys and Games   93

WORK   96

Commercial Life   96

Taverns, Bars, and Wine Shops   98

Fulleries   99

Bakeries (Pistrina)   101

Farming   103

Grapes   103

Olives   106

Flowers   106

The Larger Market: Macellum   107

Garum   109

Other Professions   109

Doctors   110

EPILOGUE   113

INDEX   115

The Nucerian Gate with Mt. Vesuvius in the distance.

INTRODUCTION

The following report provides the only eyewitness record to the eruption of Vesuvius in A.D. 79. In this letter to the historian Tacitus, Pliny the Younger describes the catastrophe and what happened to his uncle, Pliny the Elder, a renowned natural historian and Admiral of the Roman fleet stationed at Misenum.

"My uncle was stationed at Misenum, in active command of the fleet. On 24 August, in the early afternoon, my mother drew his attention to a cloud of unusual size and appearance . . . like a pine . . . for it rose to a great height on a sort of trunk and then split off into branches. My uncle ordered a boat to be made ready. As he was leaving the house he was handed a message from Rectina. . . . She implored him to rescue her from her fate. He gave orders for the warships to be launched and went on board with the intention of bringing help to many more people besides Rectina. Ashes were already falling, hotter and thicker as the ships drew near, followed by bits of pumice and blackened stones, charred and cracked by the flames: then suddenly they were in shallow water, and the shore was blocked by the debris from the mountain. . . . [The] wind was full in my uncle's favour, and he was able to bring his ship in.

"Meanwhile on Mount Vesuvius broad sheets of fire and leaping flames blazed at several points. My uncle tried to allay the fears of his companions by repeatedly declaring that these were nothing but bonfires left by peasants or empty houses on fire. . . . Then he went to rest. . . . By this time the courtyard giving access to his room was full of ashes mixed with pumice-stones, and if he had stayed in the room any longer he would never have got out. He was wakened and joined the rest of the household who had sat up all night. They debated whether to stay indoors or take their chance in the open, for the buildings were now shaking with violent shocks, and seemed to be swaying to and fro as if they were torn from their foundations. Outside there was the danger of falling pumice-stones, even though these were light and porous. . . . [A]fter comparing the risks, they chose the latter."

Later that day Pliny the Elder was overcome by poisonous fumes. He was one of the thousands of victims claimed by Mount Vesuvius. In another letter to Tacitus, Pliny the Younger describes his own flight at dawn the morning of this uncle's death.

"[D]arkness fell, not the dark of a moonless or cloudy night, but as if the lamp had been put out in a closed room. You could hear the shrieks of women, the wailing of infants, and the shouting of men. Many besought the aid of the gods, but still more imagined that there were no gods left. . . . At last the darkness thinned. . . . We were terrified to see everything changed, buried deep in ashes like snowdrifts."

DEATH & DISCOVERY

Where did all the people go?

This is a ghost town called Pompeii. The buildings have no roofs. The walls are missing or damaged. Staircases lead nowhere. The city is silent. Why does Pompeii look like a war-torn city? Look above the buildings and trees. A mountain looms over the city— a mountain called Mt. Vesuvius. This is no ordinary mountain. Mt. Vesuvius is a volcano. On August 24, A.D. 79, Mt. Vesuvius transformed Pompeii from a lively, crowded city into a ghost town.

A Thriving Roman Town

Nineteen hundred years ago Pompeii was a small, bustling Roman city. It was primarily a commercial and agricultural town. It was probably similar to many small towns throughout the vast Roman Empire.

In A.D. 79 Pompeii was a prosperous town of ten to twenty thousand people. It was ideally situated as a center of trade. It lay on the only route between the fertile valleys of the region known as Campania and the sea. Pompeii had two good ports: one on the Bay of Naples (which is part of the Mediterranean Sea) and the other one on the Sarno River. Pompeii traded with other small Roman towns nearby, as well as with distant empires such as Egypt and Spain.

A wealth of natural resources also contributed to Pompeii's pros-

(Previous page) In A.D. 79 this street was crowded and noisy. People wearing togas and sandals walked along the sidewalks. Mules brayed. Children played. Merchants peddled their goods. Carts carrying fish, pottery, or jugs of wine clattered over the stones.

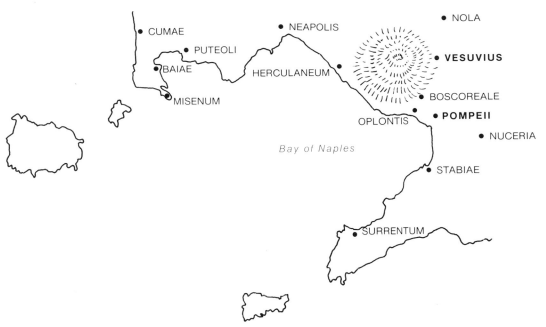

(Top) Pompeii was one of many small Roman towns dotting the coastline of the Bay of Naples in a part of southern Italy called Campania.

(Bottom) The Roman Empire about A.D. 69.

perity. The sea provided Pompeians with one of their favorite foods—fish—and one of their most popular products—garum, a spicy sauce made from fish entrails. Its fertile volcanic soil and mild climate helped make Pompeii a successful agricultural center. Pompeians raised grain, grapes, olives, sheep, and flowers. They made and sold bread, wine, olive oil, wool, perfume, and garlands of flowers.

In A.D. 79 Pompeians planted vineyards and grazed their sheep on the slopes of Mt. Vesuvius. They did not know Mt. Vesuvius was an active volcano. It had not erupted in so long that its sides were green with vegetation.

4

(Above) Painting of Mt. Vesuvius made before the eruption in A.D. *79, showing one peak and trees covering its sides.*

(Opposite) Because of the splendid climate and scenery of Campania, rich Romans built luxurious villas like this one at the town of Oplontis near Pompeii.

Earthquake of A.D. 62

The first signs that Mt. Vesuvius was waking up came in A.D. 62. Pressure building beneath the volcano caused a violent earthquake in southern Italy. Damage in Pompeii was extensive. Roofs caved in. Columns crumbled to the earth. Statues crashed to the ground. A major water reservoir cracked open and flooded the streets of Pompeii. The energetic Pompeians immediately began rebuilding the city. Most homes were repaired and redecorated in the first few years. Seventeen years after the earthquake many temples and other public buildings were still being rebuilt.

The Temple of Jupiter, badly damaged by the earthquake of A.D. 62, had not been repaired and probably looked like this in A.D. 79.

Mt. Vesuvius erupting in March 1944, as photographed from a U.S. Navy plane.
(Credit: *U.S. NAVY.*)

Mt. Vesuvius Blows Its Stack

In late August of A.D. 79 the earth began to rumble and shake. Streams and well water disappeared as if dried up by some great heat. The sea heaved and churned. Animals became restless. Mt. Vesuvius was about to blow its stack.

At about one o'clock on the afternoon of August 24, A.D. 79, Pompeians were eating lunch or preparing to rest. Suddenly a deafening sound was heard. The top of Mt. Vesuvius blasted off. Expanding gases from deep inside the volcano hurled volcanic ash and red-hot stones thousands of feet into the air. Fountains of fire, smoke, and molten lava gushed out of the mouth of the volcano. Violent earthquakes shook the ground for miles around. Volcanic

Other towns and villas near Pompeii were buried by the eruption in A.D. 79. The mosaic floor in the atrium of a house in nearby Herculaneum was pushed out of shape by the weight of the lava.

dust covered the sky and completely blotted out the sun. The day became darker than the blackest night. The sea roared and rose up in great waves.

Volcanic matter shot out of Mt. Vesuvius, forming a giant mushroom-shaped cloud that rose twelve miles into the sky. The cloud spread over Pompeii and the Sarno plain and released a rain of ash and lava stone. Volcanic debris accumulated at the rate of six inches an hour. It piled on top of roofs until they crashed under its weight. It fell until the city was covered under a blanket twelve feet thick. The harbor became so filled with volcanic deposits that no ships could sail.

Pompeii Dies at 6:30 A.M., August 25

Eleven hours after the first explosion, the force of the eruption weakened. The twelve-mile-high column of debris above the volcano collapsed, sending a glowing avalanche of ash, stone, and superheated gases roaring down the west side of the volcano.

During the night and next morning the column collapsed five more times—each time causing another fiery surge to roar down the volcano at speeds of 60 to 180 miles per hour and temperatures above 212°F. Three of these surges came close to Pompeii, but did not reach the walls. At about 6:30 A.M. on August 25 the fourth surge blasted through Pompeii at hurricane speeds. It blew off roofs and knocked people over. The hot, ash-filled air clogged their lungs and snuffed out their lives. The poisonous gases that rose out of the depths of the volcano seeped into their rooms and asphyxiated them. And still the ash kept falling. When it finally stopped, only the tips of roofs that had not caved in could be seen.

Death

The people of Pompeii were terrified. Some grabbed the nearest donkeys and headed for the city gates. Some ran to the sea. Some escaped. Many did not.

Some Pompeians decided it was too dangerous to leave their homes. Eighteen members of the House of Diomedes ran to the cellar. They clung to each other as they waited for the ash to stop falling. Poisonous gases seeped into their hideaway, and they all died.

The doorkeeper at the House of Menander covered his small daughter's head with a pillow and then quietly waited for the end.

A muleteer huddled by the gymnasium wall. He covered his face to keep out volcanic dust and ash.

A guard dog chained up in the House of Vesonius Primus struggled frantically to free himself. But the ash kept falling, and soon he was completely buried under many feet of ash and stone.

Recapturing the Past in Plaster

In 1864 Giuseppe Fiorelli, a brilliant archaeologist, made a startling discovery. He knew that the ash that covered Pompeii hardened around the fallen bodies and other organic things. When an animal, plant, or other object decayed, it left a space, or cavity, in the hardened lava. Fiorelli poured liquid plaster into the cavity. He let the plaster harden. He then broke away the lava around the plaster, leaving a cast of the figure or object exactly as it had been buried. Fiorelli's method of casting captured the drama of the last moments of life in Pompeii.

(Top) Cast of a man found in the House of Rufus.

(Bottom) Casts of members of the House of Diomedes.

10

(Top) Cast of one of thousands of victims found so far in Pompeii.

(Bottom left) Cast of a guard dog.

(Bottom right) Cast of a Pompeian muleteer holding a cloth to his mouth to keep out poisonous fumes and volcanic ash.

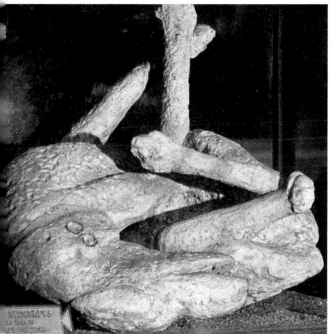

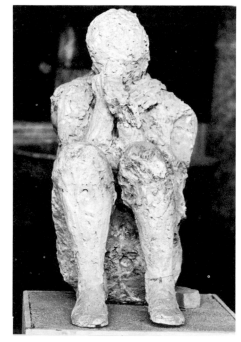

Buried and Soon Forgotten

In the first few days after the eruption some people tried to dig through the ash to get to their houses. Looters stole sculptures, jewelry, and other objects of value. But it was dangerous to dig into the buried city. Pockets of poisonous gases still lay trapped under the lava. Soon no one returned to Pompeii. Grass grew over the site. People called the area *Civitas*, which means ancient city. It was not long before they forgot that the thriving city of Pompeii had ever existed.

How was Pompeii discovered?

The First Clue

Years passed. Centuries passed. For more than 1500 years Pompeii lay buried and forgotten. In 1594 Pompeii was *almost* discovered by accident. Workmen digging an underground channel to bring water from the Sarno River to a rich man's villa came across bits and pieces of ruined buildings. They even found an inscription with the words *decurio Pompeiis*. This was an important clue, but not even the architect in charge, Domenico Fontana, connected the words with the lost city of Pompeii. Pompeii remained buried and undiscovered for another 154 years.

Herculaneum Is Discovered

In 1709 the Austrian Prince d'Elbeuf had a well dug on his property in the town of Resina. By accident the prince's workmen dug into the ancient theater of Herculaneum, a nearby city that was buried by the same eruption that destroyed Pompeii. Prince d'Elbeuf made a world-shattering discovery—he rediscovered Herculaneum. But the prince was not interested in his find for its historic value. He was interested only in the treasures he could collect to decorate his villa. By tunneling into the theater and looting it, the prince's workers destroyed the best-preserved theater of ancient times.

However, excavation at Herculaneum was soon abandoned. The mud-lava that covered this seaside resort had hardened into stone too difficult to excavate.

Digging Out Pompeii

The excitement inspired by the discoveries at Herculaneum encouraged scholars to look for other ruins nearby that might reveal treasures of their own. In 1748 a Spanish engineering officer, Roque de Alcubierre, dug through the dirt and hardened ash covering Pompeii and reached the Temple of Fortuna Augusta. Pompeii was officially rediscovered, and excavations began in earnest. In 1763 an inscription including the words *Res publica Pompeianorum* was uncovered near the city wall. This evidence confirmed that Civitas was indeed the long-lost Pompeii.

Map of Pompeii

The first excavators were careless. They dug through thirty feet of earth and hardened ash with no care for what lay underneath. They destroyed many objects that gave clues about the Roman way of life. These early excavators had no interest in Pompeii for what it told about the past. They wanted only to take paintings, sculptures, mosaics, and other beautiful objects for private collections.

1. Bakery of Modestus	10. Hall of Decuriones	19. House of the Orchard	28. Macellum	36. Temple of Lares
2. Basilica	11. Hall of Duoviri	20. House of Rufus	29. Small Palaestra	37. Temple of Venus
3. Building of Eumachia	12. House of the Centenary	21. House of Sallust	30. Small Theater	38. Temple of Vespasian
4. Central Baths	13. House of the Faun	22. House of the Silver Wedding	31. Stabian Baths	39. Triangular Forum
5. Doric Temple	14. House of the Golden Cupids	23. House of the Surgeon	32. Temple of Apollo	40. Villa of Cicero
6. Forum Baths	15. House of the Large Fountain	24. House of the Tragic Poet	33. Temple of Fortuna Augusta	41. Villa of Diomede
7. Fullery of Stephanus	16. House of the Marine Venus	25. House of Vesonius Primus	34. Temple of Isis	42. Villa of Julia Felix
8. Gladiator's Barracks	17. House of Menander	26. House of the Vettii	35. Temple of Jupiter	43. Villa of Mysteries
9. Hall of Aediles	18. House of the Moralist	27. Large Theater		

Map of Pompeii.

Fortunately, in the 1860s the archaeologist Fiorelli instituted a scientific method for excavating Pompeii. He divided the city into regions. Every block and every doorway had a number. Digging was done methodically from the surface of the earth downward— slowly and carefully. Every object was numbered and catalogued. Paintings were left where they were found. In this map of Pompeii you can see the way Fiorelli divided the city into blocks and regions. Notice how much of Pompeii is still buried after more than two hundred years of excavation. Beneath this crust of lava, Pompeii still has many secrets to tell. Secrets and clues that will increase our understanding of Roman life remain to be discovered.

(Top) It has taken archaeologists years of studying thousands of pieces of evidence to bring Pompeii to life.

(Bottom) Fragments of wall paintings are pieced together during restoration of the House of Rufus.

Why are Pompeii and Herculaneum so important?

The rediscovery of Pompeii and Herculaneum ignited the imagination and interest of people the world over. In fact, discoveries in Pompeii, Herculaneum, and other small Roman towns and villas at the base of Mt. Vesuvius continue to make headline news. Why?

Roman heritage is our heritage. The Romans came into contact with many different peoples. They incorporated the best aspects of many civilizations into their own culture, which they spread throughout the world they conquered. We are the inheritors of this culture. Roman law is the basis of Western law. We read stories based on Roman myths. We construct buildings patterned after Roman temples.

Pompeii provides a window into our past. Over the years, buildings deteriorate or are destroyed. Objects decay and turn to dust. New objects replace the old. The past is slowly erased and forgotten. Not so in Pompeii. The ash that destroyed Pompeii also preserved it exactly as it was on August 24, A.D. 79.

Bringing Pompeii to Life

When Mt. Vesuvius buried Pompeii and the small towns nestled around its base, it preserved a wealth of clues about Roman life. Cooking utensils, furniture, tools, jewelry, games, food, casts of bodies, plant roots, wooden doors and gates, and paintings and graffiti covering walls of buildings and tombs are but some of the millions of clues. Archaeologists study these clues to learn what a Roman town of the first century A.D. was like. For example, to understand the Pompeian political scene, archaeologists had to translate more than three thousand election notices they found painted and scratched on walls. To visualize the contests in the Amphitheater, archaeologists studied the graffiti announcing the games; the paintings, sculptures, and mosaics of gladiators found in homes and tombs; and the armor discovered in the gladiators' barracks.

(Below, left) Painting of cupids tasting wine depicts a real-life activity of ancient Pompeians.

(Below, right) Graffiti indicating oil was sold here.

(Opposite, top left) Wooden cradle preserved by airtight mud-lava in Herculaneum.

(Opposite, top right) Jewelry box, hairpins, comb, earrings, and mirror.

(Opposite, bottom) Physician's balance used to weigh medications.

INSIDE THE WALLS

Pompeii in A.D. 79

Pompeii is an empty city of ruins today, but in A.D. 79 it was a port city of ten to twenty thousand people. People from all over the Roman Empire came here to trade. You would have heard them chattering in many different languages—Latin, Greek, Egyptian, Oscan, Hebrew. Their clothes would have looked strange to you. Pompeian citizens wore togas and sandals. Slaves—and there were many of them—wore short coverings called tunics. The buildings and statues were painted with bright colors and often gaily decorated. You would have seen writing all over the building walls. Beautifully painted letters in black, red, or white spelled out words in Latin or Oscan. Two thousand years ago you would have visited a noisy, lively, colorful city.

Slaves

The majority of people in Pompeii were slaves and former slaves. Slaves were prisoners captured in wars with other empires. Some were of high birth and were more refined and educated than their masters.

Slaves did almost all the work in Pompeii. They stoked the fires that heated the baths. They turned the mills that ground flour to make bread. Carpenters, bricklayers, and plumbers were slaves. Doctors, teachers, artists, musicians, and secretaries were slaves. Artists, teachers, copyists, and the tutors of patrician boys were generally slaves of Greek origin.

A master could treat his slaves any way he wished. He could work them to

(Previous page) View of Pompeii from a lookout tower on the wall. The road leads to the Forum.

death without fear of prosecution. However, most slave owners were not so in-humane. Some masters taught their slaves trades. Some gave them money to start businesses. Some treated them as if they were their own children. But no matter how well treated, a slave was not free.

Slaves were able to gain their freedom. They could buy freedom with money they had accumulated from tips or outside jobs. Some masters freed their slaves out of gratitude or friendship. Former slaves were called freedmen.

The population of Pompeii included many freedmen and sons of freedmen. In the years before A.D. 79 freedmen had accumulated enough wealth to own many of the finest mansions in Pompeii.

Major Features of Pompeii

Site

The city of Pompeii has an irregular shape because it was built on the tip of a lava flow. Perched high on this volcanic ridge, 130 feet above the sea, Pompeii dominated the countryside. Because of its ideal location for trade and agriculture, many empires fought to rule Pompeii. Over its nine-hundred-year history, Pompeii was occupied by Greeks, then Etruscans, then Samnites, and finally by the Romans in 80 B.C.

Wall and Gates

The dark line on the map represents the wall that the Greeks built around the city. Both its elevated site and the wall provided Pompeii with important defensive advantages. In A.D. 79 Pompeii no

(Above) The wall surrounding Pompeii was 20 feet thick and 26 feet high. It had 12 lookout towers.

(Opposite) Herculaneum Gate. Pedestrians walked under side arches. Central arch (now missing) was for animals and light carts.

24

longer needed the wall. As a Roman colony, it was protected by the mightiest army in the world. However, the wall was left standing. The future was too uncertain to tear it down.

The eight gates in the wall were the only ways to get into and out of the city. They were noisy and congested. Carts, heavily loaded with goods, slowly rumbled through them. Venders loudly hawked their wares at stalls along the roads. Pedestrians stopped to browse, bargain, or buy before they passed through the gates into the city.

Street Plan

The street plan of Pompeii is quite similar to that of a modern American city. The streets intersect to form narrow rectangular blocks called *insulae.* Some blocks were completely covered by one large home. Other blocks contained many smaller homes. Still other blocks contained mixtures of homes and shops. Except for the large open public areas, every inch of space in Pompeii is covered with buildings.

Public Areas

Three large public areas stand out on the map. In the southwestern corner is the Forum, or town center—a large square around which are grouped government buildings, temples, and markets. The public sports center with its tremendous gymnasium (Large Palaestra) and stadium (Amphitheater) is located at the eastern corner. The theater district, which includes both a large and a small theater, occupies part of a public area on the southern side. The remains of a Greek Temple and Greek Forum (Triangular Forum) and barracks for gladiators are also located here.

Streets of Tombs

Roman law forbade burial or cremation within the city walls. Tombs lined the busy roadways approaching the city gates. Clusters of vender stalls were interspersed among the monumental stone or marble tombs.

(Top) The Street of Tombs outside the Nucerian Gate was once filled with mule-drawn carts, vendors, travelers, and loiterers.

(Bottom) Commercial streets were bustling and crowded. Shops had open fronts, and wares were displayed on shelves and hung from doorways. Wall signs advertised merchandise and prices.

A Walk Through the Streets of Pompeii

As you walk along the streets in Pompeii, you often feel closed in by walls pressing in on both sides. The streets are generally narrow—about ten feet wide. Even the main streets are no more than twenty-eight feet wide, the width of a typical narrow two-lane American street. Narrow streets make sense in a Mediterranean climate. In the hot summer when the sun sizzles, buildings lining the street create shade. In the cold, damp winter, buildings block the wind.

The sidewalks are high—with good reason. Pompeii had no garbage trucks and only a primitive sewer system. The streets were often filled with rainwater or the smelly garbage that people threw from their houses. Pigs and dogs wallowed in the scraps or bran

(Opposite) A typically narrow Pompeian street. Cart wheels made the deep ruts in the lava stones paving the street.

(Top) A continuous stone wall broken only by a few small windows is typical of residential neighborhoods.

(Bottom) One of the few storm sewers in Pompeii; it was designed to carry water from the Forum.

that bakers discarded in the street. People avoided walking in the street by crossing on the stepping stones in the middle.

Roman Engineering Genius: Pompeii's Water System

A plentiful supply of fresh water was vital to the Pompeians. Not only did they use running water in their homes, they needed water to supply tremendous bathhouses and elaborate fountains. The Romans built extensive collection, distribution, and storage systems to ensure adequate water supplies to all their cities.

Each day an aqueduct brought thousands of gallons of water to Pompeii from Avellino eighteen miles away. The water was collected and stored in the Castellum Aquae just outside the wall near

(Opposite) The aqueduct that brought water to Pompeii probably looked like this 2000-year-old Roman aqueduct in southern France. Aqueducts were part of the water distribution system that crisscrossed the Roman Empire.

(Top right) Castellum Aquae, where water for Pompeii was collected, stored, and distributed.

(Bottom left) Water tower. Throughout Pompeii, water was stored on top of 20-foot high towers like this.

(Bottom right) Inside Castellum Aquae, cement forms directed water through three openings for distribution to various sections of the city.

the Vesuvian Gate. Here it was divided into thirds and directed to various parts of the city. Lead pipes hidden beneath the streets and inside building walls carried water into the houses and their gardens, the public fountains found at most street intersections, the large public baths, and the swimming pools.

In Pompeii's semitropical climate thirsty people and animals found relief at the public fountains. Poor families whose houses had no running water came here to fill their clay jugs (*amphorae*).

(Opposite) A public water fountain was located at almost every intersection. Lead pipes hidden beneath the streets carried water to the fountains.

(Top right) Water valves, located at street corners, could be turned with keys to stop water flow to pipes of an entire city block so repairs could be made. The valves are almost identical to those we use today.

(Bottom) Decorative floor tile is lifted to reveal lead pipe that brought water into the house.

PUBLIC LIFE

The Forum: The Heart of a Roman City

The Forum was the focus of the social, political, commercial, and religious life of every Roman town. Built to impress the public with the power of the city and its rulers, the Forum consisted of immense government buildings, temples, and a market, grouped around a large open square.

In Pompeii, the Forum was enclosed on three sides by a two-story colonnade. On the northern side stood the majestic Temple of Jupiter flanked by two triumphal arches. Three municipal buildings—the headquarters of the city mayors, their assistants, and the city council—stood at the southern side. Statues of Roman emperors and the leading citizens of Pompeii were mounted on pedestals and lined the square.

The Forum, so silent now, was once alive with activity. On a typical day, merchants set up tables or blankets and spread out their wares in the large square. Shoppers gathered around the tables. Perhaps they picked out a copper pot or iron utensil. Some bought fruit or bread. Children played hide-and-seek among the brightly colored columns. Scribes wrote letters for the illiterate. People crowded in front of the bulletin board, where announcements of slave auctions, lost property, police regulations, and court

(Previous page) The Forum. Portico and colonnade in front of the Basilica.

(Opposite, top) The Forum as it may have appeared before the earthquake of A.D. 62.

(Opposite, bottom) In A.D. 79 the Forum may have looked much as it does in this 1984 photograph. The damage caused by the earthquake of 62 was still being repaired when Vesuvius buried Pompeii.

sentences were painted. Some gathered around a large podium called the *suggestum* to hear politicians make speeches.

Government

The form of government and the constitution of Pompeii were similar to those found in other Roman colonies from England to Syria. Roman colonial government succeeded largely because it combined strong centralized control with democratic self-government on local matters.

Duoviri, Aediles, and Decuriones

In Pompeii, male citizens elected two mayors called *duoviri* to head the city council. Duoviri were in charge of government finances, local justice, and elections. To assist them, two elected junior magistrates (*aediles*) supervised the public works—the roads, public baths, and markets. The aediles also ran the games in the Amphitheater. A city council composed of one hundred wealthy freeborn citizens with property helped the duoviri and aediles run the city. *Decuriones*, as they were called, were chosen for life by members of the city council. City officials were the most powerful people in Pompeii.

City officials received no salaries. In fact, they were expected to spend large amounts of their own money on the city. Both the Small Theater and the Amphitheater were built by the duoviri C. Quitius Valgus and M. Porcius. The games in the Amphitheater were often financed by city officials with their own funds. This "generosity" ensured their popularity with the voters.

38

(Top) The office of the Aediles (junior magistrates).

(Bottom) The Curia (city council).

The Basilica (built about 100 B.C.) was the legal and business center of the city. Pompeians came here to learn news of the city and exchange gossip.

Basilica and the Law

Rome provided Pompeii with an excellent legal system—in fact, modern Western law is based on Roman law. The Romans created a large body of laws affecting every aspect of life. Some of the more noble principles taken from Roman law are that all persons are equal in the eyes of the law and that a person is innocent until proven guilty. Law was the most highly respected profession. (Doctors, actors, and architects received little or no respect.) Lawyers were not paid for defending clients. This was considered part of their public duty.

Law courts and business offices were located in the Basilica, one of the oldest and most important public buildings in the Forum. From the early hours of the morning the large central courtyard

40

was in a constant state of motion. Lawyers and their clients rushed into the law courts. Bankers and businessmen hurried to their offices.

It was here that a young boy began his political career—first by observing court cases, then by speaking out in court. After establishing a reputation in the courtroom, he might run for public office.

Business Transactions

In 1875, 154 business receipts in the form of wax tablets were found in a wooden box in the home of the wealthy auctioneer L. Caecilius Jucundus. These tablets, about three by five inches in size, were made of two strips of wood joined together at one edge. The inner surfaces were hollowed out and filled with wax. Jucundus or his secretary would scratch the receipts for loans and rent payments into the wax of the two tablets. These tablets were then tied together and sealed so no one could tamper with the information. Witnesses stamped their seals onto the wood backing. A third tablet fastened to the first two summarized the business trans-action. These bound receipts provide excellent insights into Roman business.

Graffiti

Pompeians had no paper as we know it. Their books were made of blocks of wax or rolls of papyrus, a paperlike material made of reeds. Both wax and papyrus were limited in supply and cumbersome to use. However, the Pompeians had much to write about. So, to express themselves, announce games and activities, publicize their candidates, they used writing surfaces readily available—

walls! No vertical surface was sacred. They often painted or scratched notices into the sides of tombs and the walls of the most elegant homes. These graffiti provide invaluable insights into all aspects of everyday Roman life. From the most private love poem to a political advertisement for government office, we see Pompeians as real people with concerns, joys, fears, and a sense of humor. All this is preserved in their graffiti.

Writing on the Walls

A not-so-friendly note: "Samius to Cornelius: go hang yourself."

An admirer's wish: "Health to you, Victoria, and wherever you are may you sneeze sweetly."

A house owner's warning: "No place for loafers here; move along!"

Lost-and-found notice on a tomb: "If anybody lost a mare with a small packsaddle, November 25, let him come and see Quintus Decius Hilarus. . . ."

An ancient observer's comment on the graffiti on the Basilica walls: "I am astounded, O wall, that you do not crash under the weight of all this trash."

From graffiti we learn that money was paid to the city to rent refreshment stalls at the games. Fines were paid for bribery, illegal candidacy, neglecting oaths of office, selling city property, and damaging sacred sites, roads, or water pipes.

Election Graffiti on the Walls

More than three thousand notices found on walls in Pompeii tell us about elections in the city. Only male citizens could vote, and

Graffiti. Professional sign painters painted election slogans and notices of amphitheater events in red, black, or white letters on walls of houses and shops.

only those who owned property could run for office. But the whole population, including slaves and women, enthusiastically entered into campaigns during election times.

Every group supported its candidates with election graffiti. "The barbers recommend Trebius for the office of aedile." "Do make Verus aedile, perfumers, elect him, I beg of you." "The chess players ask you to vote for L. Popidius Ampliatus for aedile."

One wonders if the opposition painted the grafitti indicating that Vatia is recommended by "sneak thieves," "the whole company of late drinkers," and "everyone who is fast asleep."

Religion

Pompeians, like other Romans, believed in many gods. They invented gods to explain what confused or frightened them—lightning, volcanoes, earthquakes, the seasons. They created myths to explain acts of nature. Plants died, leaves fell off trees, and the world became cold because the goddess Persephone spent six months in the underworld. Day was caused by the sun god Apollo riding across the sky in a chariot.

To Romans, the gods were immortal—they lived forever—but they had human strengths and weaknesses. They were completely unpredictable. They angered quickly. On a whim, these superhuman beings might bring a pestilence to Pompeii's vineyards, cause businesses to fail, or even cause an earthquake. Romans made offerings and sacrificed animals to appease the gods. They built

Venus, goddess of love, was Pompeii's patron goddess. Her image was found throughout Pompeii, as (opposite) on a garden wall, and (top right) in a private bathhouse.

(Bottom) Roman temple (first century B.C.) in Nimes, France. The Temple of Jupiter probably looked like this before it was damaged by the earthquake of A.D. 62.

(Top left) Head of Jupiter, king of the gods, once part of a large statue in the Temple of Jupiter.

(Bottom) The Temple of Jupiter, where Rome's most important gods and goddesses, such as Jupiter, Juno, and Minerva, were worshiped.

(Opposite, left) Blue glass vase discovered in a tomb near the Herculaneum Gate. Reliefs of cupids harvesting grapes suggest the deceased owned vineyards.

(Opposite, right) Mosaic captures Pompeian philosophy: Drink and be merry today, for tomorrow you may die!

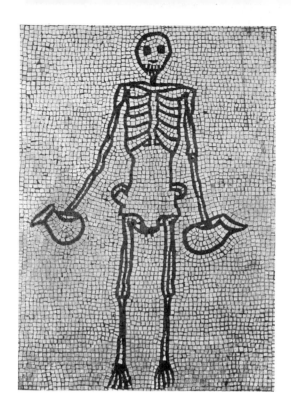

elaborate temples to flatter them. They hoped a happy god would make their business thrive, their crops grow.

The Roman religion was concerned with the here and now—success, wealth, and health. It did not teach morality, the difference between right and wrong, and was not concerned with sin or virtue.

Pompeians built elaborate tombs for themselves and their relatives to honor their lives and impress passersby. They filled the interiors with paintings and treasures. Tombs were conceived of as homes for the dead, places where their spirits could remain in touch with the living. Tombs were even built with benches for dining. Each year on the birthday and the anniversary of the death of the deceased, the family held feasts at the tomb. The Romans believed that the spirit of the dead hovered near the tomb and took

47

part in the ritual meal.

Religion was a part of everyday life. Six of the twelve grand buildings surrounding the Forum were temples. There were altars to worship gods in the streets, in the homes, and even in the snack bars.

Worship at Home

Worship at home meant more to the Pompeians than the formal ceremonies at the many public temples. The daily rituals they performed together at home created strong family bonds. Each home had at least one *larium*—a miniature temple or painting with an altar in front—to worship the household gods (*Lares*) and the spirits of the family ancestors. These gods kept the family safe, healthy, wealthy, and successful. As head of the family, the father performed the role of priest. At every evening meal the family made an offering of flowers, fruits, sacrificial cakes, incense, or an

(Opposite) Painting from the tomb of C. Vestorius Priscus shows off the family silver collection.

(Top right) Altar to worship gods in the street and (bottom) in the snack bar.

(Left) Altar (larium) to worship the household gods (Lares) and ancestors of the family (Penates) was often placed in the atrium.

(Bottom) Picture depicting rituals of the cult of Dionysus, the Greek mystery religion.

animal (usually a pig) to the small figures within the shrine. They even shared their dinner with the gods.

Oriental Religions Fill a Void

For many centuries the Roman religion fulfilled the needs of its citizens. Belief in a common system of gods and rituals gave their lives structure. It helped unify the family and the Empire. However, by the first century A.D. the Roman religion did not fully satisfy some Pompeians. It served their practical needs but did not appeal to their emotions.

As a port city open to ideas and people from all parts of the world, Pompeii was in a perfect position to be influenced by the mystery religions imported from the East. The cult of the Egyptian goddess Isis and the cult of Dionysus, Greek god of wine, were extremely popular. Eastern mystery religions, with their secret initiation rites, fasting, feasting, wild dancing, orgies, and mystic trances, offered the excitement bored Pompeians were seeking. Belief in an eternal afterlife guaranteed by some of the new religions gave converts more comfort and hope than the austere Roman religion could offer.

Popular Entertainment

The grandiose and elegant entertainment centers in Pompeii were typical of even the smallest Roman town. Pompeii had a population of only ten to twenty thousand people, and yet it had a stadium that held twenty thousand. Its Large Theater held five thousand; its Small Theater, fifteen hundred. The public gymnasium was immense, about 448 by 416 feet, was lined by majestic plane trees, and had a tremendous swimming pool in the center. The public baths, another form of Roman entertainment, were large and ornately decorated.

Theater

The Large Theater was terraced into the hollow of a hill near the Triangular Forum. Marble seats rose in semicircular tiers facing the stage. Prominent officials took the best seats in the first rows. Some, such as decuriones, had special double seats.

The stage was long and narrow. The rear wall of the stage had a permanent backdrop constructed in the form of a palace with arches, columns, niches for statues, and water gushing from fountains.

Telescoping rods raised the curtain from a slit in the stage floor. Niches in front of the stage were provided for those charged with maintaining order in the theater.

Equipped with mechanical devices to create special effects, this two-thousand-year-old stage was as sophisticated as many of its modern descendants. During a production, painted scenery in front of the backdrop could be slid to the side to reveal another scene. In addition, three-sided panels could be revolved for quick changes of scenery. Machines to create special effects were located underneath the stage. One device created the booming sounds of thunder. Another flooded the stage with water for naval battles or water scenes. A cranelike machine raised gods or heroes into the heavens or lowered them from the clouds.

The Large Theater had no roof. To protect the audience from the blazing sun, a great awning (*velarium*) was stretched over the theater. Sprays of saffron-colored water (*sparsiones*) were sprinkled over spectators to keep them cool.

52

The Large Theater, older than any extant Roman theater, was built between 200 and 150 B.C.

Pompeians loved the theater. Shows were generally rowdy, vulgar, and lowbrow. Spectators roared as they watched actors poke fun at society. Juggling, dancing, singing, and clowning—all part of a mime act—drew enthusiastic crowds.

The most sophisticated entertainment at the theater was the pantomime. The lead actor (the *pantomimus*) acted out a story using only gestures. The pantomimus was a pop hero like our modern movie and rock stars. Fans expressed their devotion to their favorite actors on many walls throughout the city. "Actius, darling of the people, come back quickly!" On a tomb: "Paris, pearl of the stage."

(Left) Sculpture of a theater mask used to decorate a garden fountain. Masks were used by actors in the Greek theater.

(Bottom) The Small Theater was reserved for entertainment on a more refined level: poetry readings, singing, and lectures. It was built with a roof, probably to improve the acoustics.

(Opposite) Amphitheater, interior view.

Amphitheater

Pompeii's Amphitheater is the oldest known amphitheater still in existence. It was built in 80 B.C., 160 years before the Roman Colosseum. The Amphitheater is a magnificent oval structure 460 feet long and 345 feet wide. It was large enough to hold the entire population of Pompeii plus visitors—twenty thousand in all.

The shows in the Amphitheater were by far the most popular entertainment in Pompeii. The shows were spectacular. They lasted continuously for several days. Sponsored by magistrates to gain popularity or votes, these shows were free of charge and heavily attended. Twenty thousand spectators cheering and screaming, trumpets blowing, horns blaring, animals growling—the noise in the stadium must have been deafening. It was probably like halftime at a football game—only more so.

The gladiator contests were the highlight of the shows in the Amphitheater. Gladiators were the superstars of Roman times. Many were loved and idolized as movie stars are today. Abundant graffiti testify to this devotion. Gladiators were slaves, prisoners of war, debtors, or criminals trained in special schools to fight one another to the death.

Gladiator contests originated in Campania many years before they became popular with the Romans. The contests were initially part of a religious ceremony honoring the death of a great chief with the sacrifice of a human life to the gods. Over the years the religious aspect gave way to pure entertainment.

Early in the morning on the day of the event, merchants began setting up wooden stands outside the great arena. People gathered in taverns and bars to bet on their favorite gladiators.

(Opposite) Amphitheater, exterior view. The outside staircases led to the upper galleries, reserved for women and slaves.

(Top right) One of many gladiator helmets found in gladiator barracks.

(Bottom left) Shoulder armor was used together with a net, trident, and dagger by some gladiators.

(Bottom right) Bronze greaves, used to protect gladiators' legs.

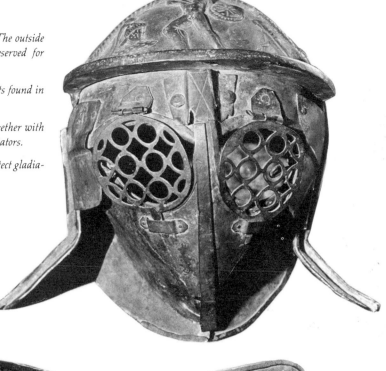

57

The games began with a grand procession through the Forum. Crowds of Pompeians followed the splendidly dressed gladiators through the city to the Amphitheater. The blare of a trumpet announced the first event: a contest between a pair of gladiators. The contests were fought to the death unless the audience interceded with a hand sign. "Thumbs up" meant life; "thumbs down" meant death. Often as many as forty gladiators were sacrificed in a day. Great metal hooks dragged the lifeless losers across the sandy Amphitheater floor.

Halftime included mock fighting and the execution of criminals. In the afternoon there were contests between animals, and between animals and men. These contests were particularly brutal because the contestants were unevenly matched. A tiger or panther might be roped together with a horse or young deer. Large numbers of helpless animals such as ostriches were slaughtered by men armed with bows and arrows. Slaves or criminals were pitted against wild beasts such as bears or lions.

Physical Fitness and Exercise

Physical fitness and exercise were of utmost importance to Romans. The main sports center was the Large Palaestra. It was tremendous—more than four acres in size—and magnificent. In the center was an immense swimming pool surrounded by majestic plane trees. Joggers of A.D. 79 ran under covered porticoes that bounded the gymnasium on three sides.

Team sports like soccer, baseball, or football had not yet been invented, but Pompeians did enjoy discus throwing, jumping, bowling, wrestling, and swimming. While the Large Palaestra was

(Top) Painting of the A.D. 59 Amphitheater riot between Pompeians and visiting Nucerians over a gladiator contest. Many Nucerians were killed or wounded. The Roman Senate punished Pompeii by closing the Amphitheater for 10 years.

(Bottom) Gladiators' Barracks, as much a prison as a home. Remains of stocks with bar and lock, used to discipline gladiators, were found in the barracks guardroom.

The Large Palaestra. The larger-than-Olympic-size swimming pool can be seen inside.

60

open to both rich and poor, smaller palaestra throughout the city catered to wealthy clients. A small palaestra near the Triangular Forum was used exclusively to train young boys in athletics.

Baths: Not Just for Keeping Clean

Among the most popular entertainment centers in Pompeii were the public baths. We think of taking a bath as a way to get clean. We shower or bathe in the privacy of our own homes. The Romans had a different idea. They built beautiful bathhouses not just as places to bathe but as places to meet friends, talk business, swim, exercise, be massaged, recite poetry, read quietly, relax, have a snack. Each public bath also included a small palaestra and swimming pool.

From two P.M., when slaves announced the opening of the baths, until late at night, when the baths closed (1328 lamps were found in the Forum Baths), Pompeians amused themselves at one of the large public or smaller private baths in the city.

In A.D. 79 bathing involved more than a casual dip in a bathtub. It was a complicated ritual that could last several hours.

The first stop was the dressing room (*apodyterium*), where a slave helped his master undress. The dressing room was beautifully decorated with red walls and a stuccoed ceiling. Cubbyholes similar in purpose to modern-day gym lockers were built into the walls. Squeezed together on benches, slaves waited while their masters went outside to exercise in the open-air gymnasium. Exercise included wrestling, throwing discus, jogging, bowling, or swimming.

Hot and sweaty from exercise, bathers came inside to the warm room (*tepidarium*) for a massage. Slaves rubbed them with oil and

61

(Above) Dressing room (apodyterium) with cubbyholes for clothes.

(Opposite, left) Strigiles, used to scrape oil and dirt off bathers' skin.

(Opposite, right) Raised floor of caldarium allowed hot air from the central furnace to circulate and warm the floor.

then scraped off the dirt and oil with curved metal scrapers called *strigiles.*

The steamy hot room (*caldarium*), which followed, was like a sauna. Here the bather worked up a sweat. After a warm bath, he was invigorated by a plunge in the cold bath (*frigidarium*).

Before leaving, the bather was massaged with oils to protect him from catching cold.

CENTRAL HEATING IN A.D. 79 In the early days the baths were warmed by bronze space heaters called braziers. In the first century B.C. Sergius Orata, a man who became rich by planting artificial oyster beds, invented a superior heating method called a *hypocaust*. The floor of the bath was raised on stacks of bricks. Hot air from the central furnace circulated under the floors between the raised bricks and in the hollow spaces between the walls to warm the rooms.

PRIVATE LIFE

Homes

Walking through a residential neighborhood in Pompeii, you would have seen no front porches, front steps, picture windows, broad green lawns, tall shade trees, or picket fences. In Pompeii, the continuous stone outer walls were only rarely broken by windows or doors. The few windows were small, high, and often barred. Private houses were built to keep strangers and burglars out and to shield those inside from the noise, odors, and heat of the outside.

The Atrium, Cool and Serene

Outside the austere facades of private homes the street was a jumble of noises, smells, and movement. As soon as visitors passed through the narrow, dark vestibule, they entered a world of light, serenity, and grandeur. The atrium was immense, often more than forty by fifty feet and twenty-eight feet high. The walls were covered with splendid murals and paintings. The floor was tiled with intricate mosaic patterns. The ceiling was often paneled or carved. This was a room designed to impress visitors with the wealth of its owner. In fact, the family treasure chest was often prominently displayed here. A portrait bust of the head of the family sometimes stood in the rear of the room.

In earlier times the atrium was the center of family life. By A.D. 79 the atrium was used as a reception room where the master of the house met his guests.

(Previous page) Peristyle of the House of the Marine Venus.

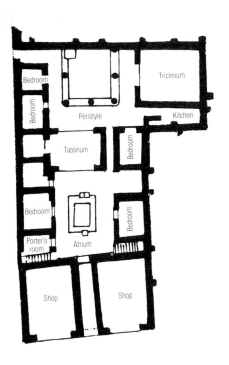

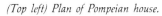

(Top left) Plan of Pompeian house.

(Top right) Imposing facade of the House of the Augustalis. Visitors to Pompeian homes were greeted by **Have** (Welcome) or **Salve Lucrum** (Hail Profit) embedded in mosaic tiles in the stone stoop at the entrance.

(Bottom right) Barred windows discouraged burglars.

(Above) Atrium of the House of the Vettii.

(Opposite) Cave Canem (Beware of Dog), a warning embedded in mosaic tiles in the floor of the entrance.

CAVE CANEM

Bringing the Outside Inside

The Pompeian house looked inward. Light, air, and rainwater entered the atrium through an opening in the roof called the *compluvium*. The water was collected in the rectangular basin (*impluvium*) in the floor below. Before the Romans colonized Pompeii, water collected in the impluvium was stored in cisterns under the house. It was then the principal supply of water for the house.

Cubiculae

In contrast to the spacious, light-filled atrium, the small rooms (*cubiculae*) grouped around the atrium were dark and stuffy. The remains of beds or couches raised on stone platforms or set into

alcoves indicate that these rooms were used as bedrooms or sitting rooms. Colorful wall paintings added some cheer to these dreary, often windowless rooms.

Tablinum

Behind the atrium was the formal reception room (*tablinum*), where the master probably met with his *clientes*, men who flattered and ran errands for rich or prominent patrons in return for food or money. The tablinum could be closed off from the atrium by a curtain or a folding wooden partition. Many of the doors in ancient Pompeii slid in grooves or folded or swung on pivots exactly like our modern doors. The tablinum in most houses opened onto a light-filled colonnaded courtyard garden, the peristyle.

Peristyle

The light flooding into the peristyle brightened the entire house. The peristyle was an open-air garden inside the house. Peristyles were private miniparks filled with bubbling fountains, pools, statues of goddesses, cupids, swans, and artistic arrangements of trees, shrubs, and flowers. Not only were they the pride of the Pompeian houses, they provided an important source of light and air to otherwise dark interiors.

(Top) Bedrooms (cubiculae). Remains of a wooden bed in Herculaneum. Slats supported mattresses stuffed with straw or wool. Panel behind the bed served as a barrier against the cold.

(Bottom) Wooden folding doors separated the tablinum from the atrium.

(Above) Peristyle of the House of the Vettii has been recreated as it appeared in A.D. 79. Lead pipe carried water to plants and garden fountains.

(Opposite) Tiny garden in light well of the House of Favius Amandio.

72

Re-creating Ancient Gardens

Using Fiorelli's method of making casts, archaeologist Wilhelmina Jashemski has determined which plants grew in Pompeian gardens. When the plants buried by Vesuvius decayed, they left cavities in the hardened lava. Jashemski filled these cavities with cement. The roots of each type of plant are distinctive. She studied the casts as well as carbonized seeds and pollen grains recovered from the volcanic debris to determine the types and locations of plants in each garden.

Many homes were not large or elegant, but no matter how humble, every Pompeian house had a garden. Homes too small for a real garden had one painted on an interior wall.

The family ate in the garden. They prayed in the garden. Women wove in the garden, and children probably sailed boats in the garden pools. The open-air peristyle brought light and air to the rooms built around it. It is no wonder the peristyle replaced the atrium as the center of family life.

Dining Rooms (Triclinia)

Pompeian homes often had several dining rooms, which were used according to the weather or the season. Pompeians dined in a reclining position while leaning on one elbow, a practice the Romans adopted from the Greeks. They ate on a three-sided couch called a *triclinium*. (They also called the dining room a triclinium.) Usually three people reclined on each side of the couch. Guests were arranged on the crowded, cushioned triclinium according to their social importance. Slaves reached over the nine diners to serve food and remove plates, wipe fingers clean, and supply napkins on demand.

DINING ETIQUETTE Dining was a ritual with correct rules of behavior. As guests arrived, a slave reminded them to enter the dining room on their right foot. Crossing the threshold on the left foot was bad luck. Rules painted on the dining-room walls of the House of the Moralist listed the dos and don'ts of proper dining etiquette.

The slave shall wash and dry the feet of his guest; a napkin shall protect the cushions (on the triclinium), and care shall be taken with the linen.

Cast not lustful glances and make not eyes at another man's wife; be chaste in speech.

Refrain from anger and insolent language if you can; if not, return to your own house.

(Top) Triclinium in the House of the Moralist. Rules of dining behavior were painted on the walls.

(Bottom) Summer triclinium. Guests enjoyed the soft evening breezes and dancing water of mosaic fountains while they ate.

A THREE- TO SEVEN-COURSE FEAST Dinner began in the late afternoon. The first course, an appetizer, might be eggs or asparagus or sow's udder in tuna sauce. The second, or main, course might be pigeon cooked in a stew of melons, dates, honey, and wine or a roast boar stuffed with live thrushes. The dessert course might be fruit or a pastry. Extravagant dinners might consist of as many as seven courses and last until the early hours of the morning.

Between courses the guests were entertained by music—pipes, lyre, harp, or cithara—short plays, recitations, even shows by Spanish dancing girls. The dining room was lit by many small oil lamps or elegant oil lamps on stands.

(Above) Pompeian kitchen.

(Opposite) Decorative paintings illustrate the foods Pompeians ate.

Kitchen

The kitchen in the Pompeian home was small and tucked away in an out-of-the-way place. By modern standards, it was primitive. It had a sink and a stone hearth. Fires were built on top of the hearth, and charcoal was stored underneath.

Specially trained slaves did the cooking. A good cook could cost as much as three horses. Many of the utensils used in A.D. 79—colanders, ladles, spoons, and baking pans—are identical to those we use today.

Cooking Roman Style: *Patina de Rosis—Rose Pie*
ACCORDING TO APICIUS (A ROMAN COOKBOOK
WRITER OF THE THIRD CENTURY B.C.)

Take roses from the flower bed, strip off the leaves, remove the white from the petals, and put them in the mortar; pour over some broth and rub fine.

Add a glass of broth and strain the juice through the colander. Take four cooked calves' brains, skim them, and remove the nerves; crush eight scruples of pepper moistened with the juice and rub with the brains; thereupon break eight eggs; add one glass of wine, one glass of raisin wine, and a little oil.

Meanwhile grease a pan, place it on the hot ashes into which pour the above described material; when the mixture is cooked in the hot-water bath, sprinkle it with pulverized pepper and serve.

Bath

A Pompeian would never give up his afternoon in the public baths or the smaller private baths. But even though the wealthy enjoyed socializing at the public baths, they also built elegant bath complexes in their homes. These richly decorated suites usually included a hot room (caldarium) and a warm room (tepidarium) and might include a cold room (frigidarium).

Toilet

The toilet was located near the kitchen so that the pipe that brought water to the kitchen also flushed out the toilet.

Pompeians also used public latrines. Beautifully decorated marble toilet seats with arm rests were placed next to each other on a U-shaped bench.

Slave Quarters

Taking care of a mansion in Pompeii was an enormous job. A wealthy Pompeian might have had a staff of fifty slaves to take care of his house. In addition he had slaves to tutor his children, dress his wife and himself, arrange their hair, do the shopping, prepare the meals, etc. Rooms for slaves were usually found on the upper floor or in a corner of the house where space was available. Slave quarters were drab and crowded.

Artwork

Every wall of a Pompeian house was decorated with murals or frescoes. Mosaic patterns covered the floors. Sculpture was found both in the house and and in the garden.

In general, the artists who decorated Pompeian homes were Greek slaves. They painted pictures of gods and goddesses, scenes from Greek and Roman myths, buildings and landscapes both imaginary and real, gardens, and animals. They represented scenes from the theater, pictures of actors and musicians, foodstuffs waiting to be cooked, and daily life activities. They made their own versions of classic or popular Greek paintings, sculpture, or mosaics.

Roman portrait sculpture and painting were realistic. Unlike the Greeks, Romans did not idealize their subjects.

The artists of this time could paint perspective accurately. They painted panels, columns, etc., to look as if they were marble and three-dimensional. These techniques were lost for nine hundred years—from the downfall of the Roman Empire until the early Renaissance.

How to Make a Mural: Advice from Vitruvius, a Roman Architect and Engineer of the First Century B.C.

1. *Combine limestone, calcite, and sand.*
2. *Whip with sticks until thoroughly mixed and smooth.*
3. *Apply three coats to rough wall.*
4. *Prepare a mortar of powdered marble.*
5. *Whip with sticks until thoroughly mixed and smooth.*
6. *Apply three layers to the previous coats of mortar.*
7. *While damp, polish the surface with marble dust and apply the colors of the painting at the same time.*
8. *When dry, add figures and details of the painting.*
9. *To preserve the colors do the following:*
   a. *When wall is thoroughly dried out, blend very white punic wax with oil and apply to wall with a silken brush.*
   b. *Heat to the sweating point by burning coals of nutgalls close to it.*
   c. *Smooth by rubbing with tallow.*
   d. *Polish with clean cloths until painting is brilliant.*

(Opposite) Mosaics decorated floors and walls of homes in Pompeii (top) and Herculaneum (bottom).

(Above) Triclinium in the House of the Vettii brothers, wealthy merchants who had elaborately redecorated their house after the earthquake of A.D. 62. Large paintings like these were stylish at the time.

(Opposite, top left) Realistic portrait of man and wife holding scroll, wax tablet, and writing implement, as was fashionable in portrait painting of the time.

(Opposite, top right) True-to-life portrait bust of L. Caecilius Jucundus (or his father) includes wart and crooked ears.

(Opposite, bottom left) Painting of garden in a room off the peristyle of the House of the Orchard.

(Opposite, bottom right) Wall painting illustrates Roman knowledge of perspective.

The Discomforts of Home

For all its beauty, serenity, and majestic grandeur, a Pompeian house was probably not very comfortable.

The Pompeians had to rely on the structure of their houses for climate control and light. They had no electricity. The compluvium, open peristyle, thick stone walls, and marble or stone floors worked together to make the Pompeian house a cool retreat from the hot summer sun. However, when winter came, the Pompeian house had no defense against the cold. The methods of heating were primitive and ineffective. Smoky, smelly, coal-burning braziers were carried from room to room. These braziers were often works of art, but they created only a small amount of heat. Coal- or wood-burning furnaces for central heating had been invented but were seldom used in homes.

Windows were rarely covered by glass. In A.D. 79 glass was not transparent and thin. Roman glass was thick and usually clouded. Because it was scarce, its use was limited to windows in the Central Baths and a few of the finest dwellings.

Close-fitting wooden shutters kept out the cold, but they made the rooms stuffy, smelly, and totally dark. Fortunately, winters in Pompeii were short and generally mild.

Pompeians relied on the sun to light their homes. On sunny days, light streamed into the atrium and the peristyle. On overcast days or at night, light was provided by candles or beautifully crafted oil lamps. Candles were expensive and gave off little light. Oil lamps also shed a dim light, and the wicks created a cloud of smoke.

Houses were probably sparsely furnished. Among the few pieces

(Top left) Bronze oil lamp shaped like a duck. Neck provides handle.

(Top right) Wicks drawn through holes in oil-filled lamp burned to provide light.

(Bottom) Cast of wooden shutters in window of Pompeian house.

of furniture found in Pompeii were beds, couches, and tables. Couches and beds were finely carved from expensive materials, but lacked springs to make them soft and comfortable.

Making More Room

Patterns of housing were changing in Pompeii in A.D. 79. As the population expanded, the city became more and more crowded within the walls. Some people moved outside the city walls to the suburbs. Some houses within the city were subdivided to accommodate several families or a family and a small shop.

Changes in class structure also affected housing. Fine old aristocratic families were being replaced by newly rich merchants. Some of the established families left because the products of their vine-

(Above) Balconies in this house were bricked in to make more rooms.

(Opposite, left) Couch found in Herculaneum.

(Opposite, right) Three-legged tables were popular in Pompeii.

(Above) Snack bar built into the front of a hotel, formerly a private mansion.

(Opposite) Cupids play hide-and-go-seek in this 1900-year-old painting.

88

yards and olive groves could not compete with those imported from other Roman provinces. Others left because they were uncomfortable with the new lower-class leadership. Former slaves who had made great fortunes bought their mansions, often subdividing them into stores, workshops, or hotels.

Childhood

Children, like adults, left clues to their activities on the walls of Pompeii. They scratched drawings on the walls of the baths and the palaestrae. They wrote complaints about their teachers. They quoted writers they studied, such as Virgil, Homer, and Horace. They also left behind objects such as dolls, doll dishes, a doll baby bottle, writing tablets, games, jewelry. Paintings of cupids playing children's games decorated walls. From all of these clues as well as the writings of Roman authors of the times, we get a picture of a child's typical day.

Pompeian children woke at dawn or even earlier. They ate a small breakfast—bread and honey or perhaps a roll bought at a bakery on the way to school.

A boy wore a toga with a purple stripe along the edge. The gold charm, called a *bulla*, that he wore around his neck was given to him at his naming ceremony when he was nine days old. Baby girls were given these charms to protect them from harm at their naming ceremonies when they were eight days old. When a boy reached manhood at about age fifteen, he dedicated his bulla and childhood toys to the family gods. He exchanged his purple-edged toga of boyhood for a pure-white toga of Roman citizenship. When a girl married, she also dedicated her bulla and childhood toys to the family Lares.

(Left) This 1900-year-old comb made of bone looks like a modern plastic one.

(Right) Loom. Pompeian girls of all classes were taught to weave by their mothers.

Schools

School was held almost anywhere—in the upper rooms of a shop or the house of a wealthy child, even in the noisy Forum. A painting of the Forum depicts a teacher whipping a student with reeds while other students sit under the Forum portico with writing tablets on their laps. Graffiti on a column indicate that a school was also held outside in the Large Palaestra.

Teachers were always male slaves or freedmen and received little respect from their pupils. They were paid meager salaries by the students' parents rather than the state. Slaves might attend classes with their masters' children. Many girls were taught at home by their mothers. Poor children probably could not afford to attend school.

Discipline was harsh. A child scratched these words on a wall: "I was whipped for the third time." Menander, the Greek playwright, said, "A man who has not been flogged is not trained."

School began very early in the morning. So early, in fact, it was often still dark, and the children needed lanterns to light their way to school as well as to see in the classroom. The poet Juvenal complained that the lanterns' smoke blackened the students' books and also polluted the classrooms.

Children of the upper classes were always accompanied by a tutor (*paedagogus*), who was usually a Greek slave. The paedagogus taught them manners and proper behavior, as well as Greek.

Boys and some girls began school at age seven. They learned reading, writing, and arithmetic. They later learned Greek and Latin literature and rhetoric, the art of public speaking. Because public speaking was a way of becoming well known and eventually might lead to a position of power, rhetoric was essential for Pompeian boys who wanted to become leading citizens.

Pompeian children did not write on paper with a pencil as we do. They scratched words into wax-coated wooden tablets with a sharp tool called a stylus. They could rub out mistakes with the flat end of the stylus.

Their books were not like ours. The Pompeians read scrolls composed of many sheets of papyrus (a paper made from Egyptian reeds) joined together at the edges to make one long roll. Reading was awkward. The scroll was held in both hands; the right hand unrolled the scroll while the left hand rolled it up. Browsing through a scroll was impossible. Finding a passage meant unrolling an entire scroll. Fortunately, most volumes were short, but a long

Wall painting of (from left to right) wax tablet, inkwell, pen, and papyrus scroll.

book might require a hundred rolls of papyrus. Scrolls were hand-lettered by scribes with a quill pen or stylus. Ink was made from soot, resin, pitch, and octopus ink.

Pompeian children went home from school for a light lunch of bread, olives, cheese, figs, nuts, and water. They returned to school in the afternoon for a few hours before going to the public baths.

Toys and Games

Pompeian children had no organized team sports like soccer or baseball. Boys enjoyed running, jumping, playing ball, swimming, wrestling, fencing, and throwing the discus.

Pompeian children probably played games like leapfrog, hide-and-seek, and blindman's buff. Their toys were similar to our simpler toys—wooden dolls, doll dishes, tops, balls, boats, marbles, and banks.

WORK

Commercial Life

Pompeii was a thriving commercial town with 33 bakeries, 130 taverns and snack shops, 39 wool-processing plants, and countless other small industries and shops. It is remarkable that a town with such a small population and an area of only about seven square miles could support so much trade and commerce.

Industry was operated on a small scale. Bronze workers, felt makers, potters, woodworkers, and dyers set up small workshops throughout the city. Many workshops were set up in the front rooms of patrician mansions. When more space was needed, as was necessary for the cleaners and dyers of wool (fullers) and tanners of leather, an entire mansion might be converted to this new use.

In A.D. 79 Abbondanza was one of Pompeii's busiest commercial streets. From the early hours of the morning (Pompeians rose at dawn) shoppers strolled from store to store. They came to this block of Abbondanza Street to buy wool and felt garments at M. Vecilius Verecundus's workshop, or bronze tools from the workshop of Verus.

Thirsty shoppers stopped for a drink of warm wine at one of the two fast-food bars that sold hot beverages or at the two taverns down the street. A few Pompeians climbed upstairs to play chess at the home of Popidius Monanus.

(Top) Abbondanza Street as it might have appeared in A.D. 79.

(Bottom) View of Abbondanza Street from a snack bar.

(Previous page) Macellum (large market). The 12 columns in the center are all that remain of the structure that covered the fish pond.

(Left) Wooden accordion doors used to close a shop in Herculaneum are identical to modern accordion doors.

(Below) 1900-year-old dice.

(Opposite) Fast-food bar.

Taverns, Bars, and Wine Shops

In Pompeii there was a bar, tavern, or wine shop on almost every block. Customers paused to buy a drink or bowl of stew. Drinks were kept warm in the clay containers set into the counters. Glasses or cups were stored on step shelves.

Judging from drawings scratched into tavern walls and the large

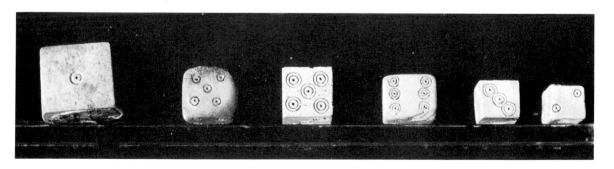

numbers of dice found, gambling was common in Pompeian inns. Taverns may have catered to a rough element of society. Higher-class travelers probably stayed at the homes of friends or at their own villas.

Hotels and taverns were plentiful at the city gates, near the Forum, and near the Amphitheater, places where visitors entered the city, did business, or enjoyed entertainment.

Fulleries

The most important industry in Pompeii was the making and cleaning of wool. Demand for wool was great because Roman togas were made of it. Pompeians bought togas at one of the many shops devoted to weaving wool and making wool garments. Unable to

(Right) Vats for cleaning wool cloth in the fullery of Stephanus.

(Opposite, top left) Screw press, used to press cloth in ancient Herculaneum, is identical to screw presses used 1700 years later in colonial America.

(Opposite, top right) Statue of Eumachia, a wealthy, prominent Pompeian who built the fullers' guild hall.

(Opposite, bottom) Doorway of the Building of Eumachia, the fullers' large and richly decorated guild hall, faces the Forum.

wash their togas at home, Pompeians took them to fullers to be cleaned and pressed.

The once-magnificent mansion of Stephanus was converted to a fullery, a laundry that cleaned, bleached, and dyed wool. Delicate wools were washed in an enlarged impluvium in the atrium. Stained cloth was cleaned by slaves who trampled it in a mixture of carbonate of soda, potash, fuller's earth, and human urine in small tubs. The cloth was then washed with other clothes in larger vats.

Bakeries (*Pistrina*)

Wheat, barley, millet, and oat bread, as well as dog biscuits, were baked fresh every morning at the thirty-three bakeries in town.

(Right) Loaf of bread, one of 81 loaves hermetically sealed for 1800 years in the oven of a Pompeian bakery. The words stamped into the top of the loaf are [C]eleris Q. grani Veri ser, meaning "(made by) Celer, slave of Quintus Granius Verus."

(Opposite, top) A bakery as it might have appeared in A.D. 79.

(Opposite, bottom) Bakery with four mills (right) and oven (left).

The large brick ovens in Pompeian bakeries are similar to modern-day pizza ovens.

Mills made of lava stone were used for grinding flour. Grain was poured into the top of the mill. Slaves or donkeys pushed wooden sticks, which fit into two square holes in the waist of the mill. As the men or animals moved around the mill, the grain was ground between the stone on top and the cone-shaped stone underneath. The flour dropped into a tray at the base of the mill. Machines for kneading dough were found in some of the bakeries.

Farming

GRAPES Grapes were Pompeii's chief crop. Although several large vineyards have been uncovered inside the walls of Pompeii and

grape vines were often grown in household gardens, most grapes were grown on the hills outside Pompeii.

Grapes were crushed in a wine press. Stored in one-hundred-gallon clay containers called *dolia*, the crushed grapes fermented into wine. Large farmhouses at the base of Mt. Vesuvius stored up to twenty-four thousand gallons of wine. Wine was brought from the farms in animal skins and then transferred to amphorae (clay jugs with pointed bottoms).

Wine from Campania was famous throughout the Roman Empire. Ancient wine amphorae bearing the names of Pompeian wine-exporting families have been found as far away as southern France. The natural historian Pliny (who died in the eruption of Mt. Vesuvius in A.D. 79) reported that one variety of Pompeian wine produced a headache that lasted until noon the next day.

104

(Right) Wine shop sign shows how wine was delivered to the many wine stores and taverns in Pompeii.

(Bottom) Reconstruction of a winepress.

(Opposite) Amphorae were large clay containers with pointed bottoms made in many sizes to hold wine, oil, grain, cereals, and garum. They were inscribed with the names of the taverns and wine shops to which they were delivered, producers of the contents, or boats on which they were shipped.

(Left) Olive press used to make olive oil.

(Opposite, top) Cupids making perfume. From right to left: Oil is extracted by crushing flowers, oils of different flowers are mixed to make perfume, perfume is sold and then offered as a gift.

(Opposite, bottom) Mensa ponderaria, table of standard measures, ensured that all measurements used in the market were fair and equal. These measurements were the same throughout the Roman Empire.

OLIVES The second most popular Pompeian product for both export and domestic use was olive oil. Olive oil was used for cooking, lighting, and massaging. The lava stone used to make olive presses and flour mills was also a popular export.

FLOWERS Flower growing was a thriving industry in Pompeii. Flowers were in demand for festivals, banquets, and funerals. Garlands of flowers decorated homes, temples, the Forum, tombs. It was customary to offer a garland of flowers to the gods at a household larium or to a guest at a dinner party. Flowers were also used to make perfume.

106

The Large Market: Macellum

Market days brought people from all over the city to the Forum. It was here in the Macellum, the largest market in the city, that shoppers found expensive gourmet foods not available in neighborhood shops. Cooks could be purchased here, too.

From the early hours of the morning, the Macellum was bustling with life—venders calling, shoppers bargaining, sheep bleating, pigeons cooing. Smells—sweet perfumes of flowers and fruit, pungent odors of wild boar and pigeons—permeated every corner of the market. Brightly colored awnings in the courtyard shaded shoppers as they moved from table to table examining goods. Customers passed under strings of garlic, sausages, and copper pots and pans hanging from the ceilings of the small shops that lined the inside walls of the Macellum. Delicacies such as figs, chestnuts, and fruits in glass bowls were displayed on the shop shelves.

Shoppers inspected fat, healthy sheep crowded together in the

pen at the northeast corner of the Macellum. Animals were bought live so they could be sacrificed to the gods before being prepared for dinner. Live fish could be selected from a fish pond set into the base of a *tholus*, a circular structure with twelve columns and a domed roof.

Pompeians loved to eat fish. They enjoyed both freshwater fish from the nearby Sarno River and saltwater fish from the Mediterranean Sea. An exotic fish might cost three times as much as a horse. Pompeians often stocked the ponds and canals in their gardens with fish.

GARUM Pompeii was famous throughout the Roman world for producing and exporting a spicy fish sauce called garum.

A Recipe for Making Garum
ACCORDING TO THE GEOPONICA (A GREEK AGRICULTURAL MANUAL)

1. *Chop small fish into tiny pieces.*
2. *Add fish eggs and the entrails of sardines and sprats.*
3. *Beat together until they become an even pulp.*
4. *Set mixture in sun to ferment, beating occasionally.*
5. *Wait six weeks or until evaporation has reduced the liquid content of the pulp.*
6. *Hang reduced liquamen in a basket with fine holes in the bottom.*
7. *Place storage jars under the basket.*
8. *Let liquid slowly drain into the jars.*
9. *Collect the liquid in the jars. This is the garum.*

Note: Use garum sparingly. It is a strong sauce with a strong smell!

Other Professions

In ancient times, the only occupations considered respectable were the ownership and management of estates and public service, both civil and military. All other work was often done by slaves or freedmen and was considered beneath the dignity of a Roman citizen. Doctors, architects, engineers, teachers, artists, actors, and writers, professionals who command much respect today, were not held in high esteem in antiquity.

Mosaic of sea creatures Pompeians enjoyed eating.

Doctors

Most doctors in antiquity probably deserved little respect. Anyone could put out a shingle and call himself a doctor. Medical training was not a requirement for becoming a physician until A.D. 222.

Surgery must have been quite advanced in A.D. 79. Scalpels, clamps, scissors, forceps, spatulas, and speculums found in a house in Pompeii are almost identical to modern surgical instruments.

Surgical tools were advanced. However, few people survived operations because Pompeians lacked anesthesia and sterile operating conditions (it was not until 1862 that the germ theory of disease was put forth by Louis Pasteur). People relied more on folklore and superstition than on doctors to cure their ills.

110

(Above) Painting of Aeneas, a Trojan hero, undergoing surgery.

(Opposite) Painting of carpenters. Carpenters, potters, wheelwrights, toolmakers, marble cutters, wood and marble inlayers, jewelers, jewelry makers, and weavers often set up shop in their homes.

EPILOGUE

Mt. Vesuvius made Pompeii into a ghost town. The city remains silent. Streets once filled with people—talking, arguing, laughing—are now disturbed only by lizards and tourists.

But we can imagine Pompeii as it once was. We still find beautiful paintings decorating its walls. Plants grow in many peristyles. Trees once more surround the Palaestra. The flour mills in the bakeries need only wooden handles and donkey power to be set in motion. We can imagine the fullers' vats filled with woolen clothing.

Pompeii is a "living" ghost town. It is a city of ruins that brings the past to life.

Streets once filled with people are now disturbed only by lizards and tourists.

Mt. Vesuvius forms a backdrop to this peaceful Pompeian scene.

114

INDEX

Page numbers in *italics* refer to illustrations.

Abbondanza Street, 96, *97*
aediles, 38, *39*
agriculture, 2, 4, 103–6
Alcubierre, Roque de, 14
altars, 48, *49, 50*
Amandio, Favius, House of, *73*
Amphitheater, 18, 26, 38, 55–58, *55, 56, 59,* 99
amphorae, 32, 104, *104*
apodyteria, 61, *62*
Apollo, 44
aqueducts, 30–32, *30*
armor, *57*
artwork, 66, 79–80, *81, 82, 83, 89*
  frescoes, 79
  mosaics, *8,* 47, 66, *67, 69,* 74, 79, *81, 109*
  murals, 66, 79, 80, *82*
  paintings, *5, 16, 18,* 48, *48, 50, 59,* 66, *76,* 79, 80, *82, 83,* 89, *89, 92, 110, 111*
  sculpture, 36, 45, 46, 54, 66, 79, *82, 100*
atria, *8,* 66, *68, 69, 70,* 73, 84
Augustalis, House of the, *67*

bakeries, 96, 101–3, *102*
bars, 56, 96, 98–99
basilica, 40–41, *40*
baths:
  private, 78
  public, 52, 61–63, *62, 63,* 78, 93
bedrooms, 69–71, *70*

books, 41, 92–93
bulla, 90
business transactions, 41
  see also trade and commerce

caldaria, 63, *63,* 78
carpenters, *110*
Castellum Aquae, 30–32, *31*
children, 89–93
  schools for, 91–93
  toys and games for, 93
city council, 38, *39*
Civitas, 13, 14
clientes, 71
climate, 4, 28, 32, 84
clothing, 22, 90, 99–101
commercial life, *see* trade and commerce
compluvia, 69
cooking, 77–78, *77*
cubiculae, 69–71, *70*
Curia, *39*

decuriones, 38, 52
d'Elbeuf, Prince, 13–14
dice, *98,* 99
dining, 74, 75–76
  see also foods
dining rooms, 74, 75–76, *83*
Diomedes, House of, 10, *11*
Dionysus, cult of, *50,* 51
doctors, 109, 110, *111*
dolia, 104

115

duoviri, 38

earthquake of A.D. 62, 6, *6, 37, 83*
elections, 38, 42–43
entertainment, 51–63, 76
    gladiator contests, 56–58, *57, 59*
    physical fitness and exercise, 58–61,
      93
    public baths, 52, 61–63, *62, 63,* 78,
      93
    theater, 26, 52–53, *53*
etiquette, for dining, *74,* 75
Eumachia, *100*
excavations:
    of Herculaneum, 13–14
    of Pompeii, 14–15
exercise, 58–61

farming, 2, 4, 103–6
fast-food bars, 96, *99*
Fiorelli, Giuseppe, 10, 15
fish, 4, 108–9, *108*
fish sauce, 4, 109
flower growing, commercial, 106
Fontana, Domenico, 13
foods, 4, 76–78, *76,* 93, 103–6, 108–9,
    108
Forum, 26, *29, 34–35,* 36–38, *37,* 58,
    91, *99*
freedmen, 23
frigidaria, 63, 78
fulleries, 96, 99–101, *100, 101*
furniture, 84–86, *86*

gambling, 98–99, *98*
games, 93
gardens, *64–65, 67,* 71–73, *72, 73,* 84
garum, 4, 109
gates, of Pompeii, *viii,* 25, *25, 26,* 32,
    99
gladiators, 56–58, *57, 59*

gods and goddesses, Roman, 44–47,
    45, 46
government, 38–41
graffiti, *18,* 41–43, *43,* 56
grapes, 103–4
Greece, influence of, 22, 23, 26, *50,*
    51, 75, 79, 91
gymnasium, public, 51–52

heating systems, 63, *63,* 84
Herculaneum, 3, 13–14, 17, *19, 70,* 98,
    100
homes, *4, 8,* 48, 66–89, *67*
    artwork in, *69,* 79–80, *81, 82, 83*
    atria in, *8,* 66, *68, 69, 70,* 73, 84
    baths in, 78
    bedrooms in, 69–71, *70*
    dining rooms in, *74,* 75–76, *83*
    discomforts of, 84–86
    furniture in, 84–86, *86*
    gardens in, *64–65, 67,* 71–73, *72, 73,*
      84
    kitchens in, 77, *77*
    making more room in, 86–89, *87, 88*
    reception rooms in, *70, 71*
    slave quarters in, 79
    toilets in, 78–79
    water system in, 69
    windows in, 66, *67,* 84, *85*
    worship in, 48–51, *50*
hotels, 99
hypocausta, 63, *63*

impluvia, 69
insulae, 26
Isis, cult of, 51

Jashemski, Wilhelmina, 73
Jucundus, L. Caecilius, 41
Juno, *46*
Jupiter, *46*

Juvenal, 91

kitchens, 77, *77*

lamps, 61, 76, 84, *85*
Lares, 48–51, *50*, 90
Large Theater, 51, *52*, *53*
laria, 48, *50*
law, Roman, 40–41
lawyers, 40–41

Macellum, *94–95*, 107–8
Marine Venus, House of the, *64–65*
market, *94–95*, 107–8
masks, theater, *54*
mayors, 38
measurements, *107*
Menander, 10, 91
mills, *102*, 103
Minerva, *46*
mosaics, *see* artwork
murals, *see* artwork

Nucerian Gate, *viii*

olive oil, 106, *106*
Orata, Sergius, 63
Orchard, House of the, 82
Oriental religions, *50*, 51

paedagogi, 91
paintings, *see* artwork
palaestrae, 26, 58–61, *60*
pantomime, 53
papyrus, 41, 92–93, *92*
perfume making, 106, *106*
peristyles, *64–65*, *67*, 71–73, *72*, *73*, 84
Persephone, 44
physical fitness, 58–61
pistrina, 101–3, *102*
plaster casts, 10, *10*, *11*

Pliny the Elder, ix, 104
Pliny the Younger, ix
Pompeii:
    agriculture in, 2, 4, 103–6
    childhood in, 89–93
    destroyed by eruption of Mt.
        Vesuvius, ix, 2, 7–13, 113
    discovery of, 13–14
    earthquake in, 6
    entertainment in, 51–63
    excavation of, 14–15
    government of, 38
    graffiti in, 41–43, *43*
    homes in, 66–89
    layout and major features of, 22–32
    legal system of, 40–41
    population of, 2, 22, 23
    public life in, 36–43
    religion in, 44–51
    Roman life illuminated by, 17–18
    site of, 2, 23
    trade and commerce in, 2, 22, 26,
        27, 36, 41, 96–110
    water system of, 30–32, *30*, *31*, *32*,
        33
Primus, Vesonius, House of, 10
professions, 109
    see also specific professions

reception rooms, *70*, 71
religion, 44–51
    gods and, 44–47, *45*, *46*, 48–51, *50*,
        51
    home worship and, 48–51, *50*
    Oriental, *50*, 51
Roman Empire, 2, *3*, 22
rose pie, 78
Rufus, House of, *11*, *16*

schools, 91–93
sculpture, *see* artwork

slave quarters, 79
slaves, 22–23, 77, 79, 89, 91
Small Theater, 38, 51, *54*
snack bars, 48, *49*, 88, 96, *99*
sparsiones, 52
sports, 58–61, 93
Stephanus, 101
storm sewers, *29*
streets, *15*, 25–30, *27*, *28*, *29*, *112*
    of tombs, 26, *27*
strigiles, 63, *63*
styli, 92, 93
suggesta, 38
surgery, 110, *111*

tablina, *70*, 71
Tacitus, ix
taverns, 56, 96, 98–99
teachers, 91, 109
Temple of Jupiter, *6*, 36, 45, 46
tepidaria, 61–63, 78
theater, 26, 52–53, *53*, *54*
togas, 90, 99–101
toilets, 78–79
tombs, 26, 47–48, *48*
toys, 93
trade and commerce, 2, 4, 22, 26, *27*,
    36, 41, 56, 96–110
  bakeries and, 96, 101–3, *102*
  farming and, 2, 4, 103–6

fulleries and, 96, 99–101, *100*, *101*
market and, *94–95*, 107–8
taverns, bars or wine shops and, 56,
    96, 98–99, *99*, *105*
  see also professions
triclinium, *74*, 75–76, *83*
tutors, 91

Valgus, C. Quitius, 38
velaria, 52
Venus, *44*, *45*
Vesuvius, Mt., *viii*, 3, 4, 5, 7, *114*
    eruption of, ix, 2, 6–13, *7*, 113
Vettii, House of the, *68*, *72*, *73*
villas, *see* homes
Vitruvius, 80

wall, around Pompeii, 23–25, *24*
water fountains, 32, *32*
water systems:
  in homes, 69
  public, 30–32, *30*, *31*, *32*, 33
water towers, *31*
windows, 66, *67*, 84, *85*
winemaking, 104, *105*
wine shops, 98–99, *105*
wool fulleries, 96, 99–101, *100*, *101*
work, 22, 96–110
    see also trade and commerce